THE MILLION DOLLAR

Barber

THE MILLION DOLLAR *Barber*

RAYMOND M. PATTERSON JR.

The Pharmacist, LLC
Saint Louis, Missouri

Published by The Pharmacist, LLC
Saint Louis, Missouri

ISBN: 978-0-578790-80-0

Printed on acid-free paper.

Cover design by Illustrious Vision.

Contents

Foreword

As I sit here and type the words to this book, I can't believe how quickly time has passed. It seems like yesterday when my mother, Anita L. Patterson, was telling me I needed to go to barber school. She said, "Son, always have you something you can do to make your own money and take care of yourself; you never know when someone will fire you from their business." It's funny how, when you get older, life starts to present a clear picture, allowing you to reflect on meaningful moments. As I take you through the many key essential factors of being a successful barber, beautician, and shop owner, I would also like for you to understand the basic principles of being successful in life. I've always been able to capture the emotion in moments from the past that were important and memorable to me. I hope you can learn from my past experiences and emotional challenges I've been faced with. The road I took to earn a million dollars was never planned, and I definitely didn't think the foundation of my economic success would come from a pair of clippers.

When I was growing up, my mother was a beautician who owned her own shop. My mother came from a financially challenged family that was not able to teach her the proper logistics of how to operate a business. During the 1940s and '50s, opportunities for African

American women to prosper and be a part of corporate America were slim to none. Though many Black people weren't given the opportunity to learn and partake in corporate America, they still owned and operated small businesses on their own. Strangely enough, the same principles implemented in the small business operations owned by Black men and women are also applicable in "Big Business." My mother would always tell me stories of how she and my dad picked cotton in order to earn money to buy clothes, food, and concert tickets. Going to Memphis to see legendary groups like The Temptations was a big deal coming from the bootheel of southeast Missouri. Even though my mom didn't own the cotton fields she worked on, she understood how to make money. My mother knew her mom and dad couldn't afford to give her what she wanted, so she monetized her physical efforts. "I hated going to the field—it was so hot—but I had to do what I needed to do if I wanted to go to the Motown Revue," she said. When I really look at the mindset it takes to go out to a hot field, pick cotton, and save your money in order to get something you want, that shows me the true meaning of commitment. What my mother and the rest of the young children picking cotton in those fields of Sikeston, Missouri, didn't recognize at that time was that they possessed the fundamental skills it took to become a boss and an entrepreneur.

So, how does a small-town girl from Sikeston learn to open and operate her own business without any formal training or college education? How does a small-town girl move from the cotton fields of Sikeston to St. Louis, Missouri, and raise three children by herself? I'll tell you how: my mother was a boss, is a boss, and raised a boss! The sacrifice, courage, commitment, and vision it took to work in 100° temperatures picking cotton in the hot sun is no different from the sacrifice, courage, and commitment it takes to become a boss and entrepreneur. What most people don't understand about true entrepreneurship is the mindset it takes in order to obtain what you want. True bosses and entrepreneurs understand that excuses mean nothing, and in business the only thing that truly matters is results. For example, if my mother would have gone out to the cotton-picking field and told the boss her tummy was hurting and she couldn't pick as much cotton, she would've gotten paid for the amount of cotton she picked, not the amount she intended to pick. Now, I'm not saying there aren't caring people in leadership positions who show empathy, sympathy, and concern for their employees; what I'm saying is that if you are going to own and operate a successful business, you need to embrace the concept of Reasons and Results (R and R).

My mother had a reason why she worked in those cotton fields, and unless she was awfully sick or incapacitated, nothing was going to stop her from getting those Temptations tickets or that outfit she wanted. A reason for her not reaching her goal could have been a stomachache, but she knew her result, or expected outcome, wouldn't have been accomplished. In business, the reason for not accomplishing your results should only be recognized as a learning tool for accomplishing the objective intended. My mother's objective was to make money, purchase Temptations tickets, buy an outfit, and go to Memphis, and that is what she did. Little did she know those same principles, morals, and values would allow her to open up her first barbershop.

In 1990 my mother opened up a barbershop after getting off of governmental assistance with little to no savings. Prior to opening up Cut Styles and More, my mother was bouncing around from job to job trying to find her niche in the workplace. Previously, she had worked at the post office and different beauty salons, opened a beauty salon, cleaned office buildings, and worked temporary jobs. I knew we were financially challenged and maybe even considered poor to some. To witness a woman hustling, taking the losses, fighting through the pain of disappointment and setbacks, and never stopping, gave me the strength to make myself successful in business and sports.

When I was 14 years old, my mother decided to move to Pontiac, Michigan, to pursue a relationship she was involved in. At the time, it seemed like the right thing to do. However, for me it was not good, considering all of my friends were in St. Louis and I was starting to make a name for myself in the football world. I was coming off of an amazing freshman year campaign and entering into my sophomore year as the starting running back at McCluer North High School in Florissant, Missouri. McCluer North was considered a powerhouse in football at the time, and I knew that once I made the starting lineup, I could write my own ticket to a big-time college football scholarship to any university I chose. So imagine how I felt when I heard these words: "Son, I'm going to be moving to Pontiac, Michigan, and you can come with me or you can stay here and live with your father or sister." Now remember, I was only 14 years old. I had never lived with my father before, my sister was only 19 years old and addicted to crack cocaine, and her boyfriend and I didn't get along at all! This was the biggest decision of my life at the time, because if I moved to Pontiac, I would have to leave all of my friends, enter a new high school, and reestablish myself as a football player. I was devastated, and so were my friends, but I couldn't be without my mother. I'm a momma's boy, y'all, so I made the move that summer.

So there I was, the light-skinned, skinny kid from Kinloch, now in Pontiac, Michigan, standing by my mother's side. The time I spent there was short-lived because the living conditions for me were very uncomfortable and frustrating. My mom's boyfriend had two sons and two of his nephews living with him as well. We all slept in the basement in two bunk beds. We were around the same age at the time, so you know we had some fun and we had some fights. Think about it: I was the son of the lady their father and uncle was dating. Therefore, there were a few moments when I had to let them know how we did it in Kinloch. You can take the boy from Kinloch, but you can't take the Kinloch from the boy. As the summer progressed, there was one particular time when one of the kids stole my money. I had starting working with the guy my mom was dating, hanging drywall. So one day, after a long day's work, I came back to the house to take a shower and simply go to bed. I was beat. I remember clearly setting my wallet down on the dresser and running up the stairs to take my shower. When I returned my money was gone. I asked and searched everyone in that house except for my mother; I was so upset I sat in the basement for two days watching *The Karate Kid* and *Rocky*.

Now trust and believe me when I tell you I loved watching *The Karate Kid*. It gave me my first lesson on how to take a girl on a date. I had never been on a date, so I told myself when I was able to go on my first date I would do exactly what Daniel-san did on his date. But watching *Rocky* at the time did something to me too. It was more than just any old movie. *Rocky* reminded me of myself. Rocky Balboa was a guy who didn't have much. He was overlooked, counted out, and not considered anyone's top prospect in life or boxing. As I watched the movie over and over, something inside of me went off at the tender age of 14. I looked at Rocky's situation: kind of poor and searching for his position in life. Rocky was about to challenge the heavyweight champion of the world in a boxing match for the world title. No one believed he had a chance. No one believed he deserved to even be in the ring with the heavyweight champion of the world, Apollo Creed, except Rocky and Mickey. Rocky lost that fight, but he earned the respect of the world for the grit, determination, and toughness he displayed. He fought with everything he had, he gave 100%, and the world was able to see he was a true champion, regardless of the outcome. After watching that movie, I knew I wanted to play in the NFL and make myself, my family, and most of all, my mother proud of me. I wasn't doing it just for me. I wasn't doing it to make a lot of money. I truly wanted to show all of the people who knew me and doubted me what an overlooked, skinny kid with no male influence in the household could do. Therefore, I told my mother I needed to go back home because I had some business to attend to. I went back to Kinloch, Missouri, and flourished as one of the top 100 high school football players in the country. I would go on to receive a scholarship, break collegiate records, make the All-American list, and play professionally overseas.

As I look back on my life, I know I was put on this earth to be a testimony for the underdogs of the world. What some people don't understand about learning is that you can learn some of your most valuable lessons from a person who has experienced struggle and actually walked the path you're trying to take. If a man is homeless on the street, don't walk past that man and think he's not knowledgeable. That homeless man probably could tell you how he became homeless, and you could take that information and use it to your advantage. You would at least know what not to do, and that is a very powerful thing to know! Because of my experience in starting from the bottom and making it to the top, then falling back to the bottom again, I've earned the right to share my story with anyone who's trying to accomplish a dream or goal. If you are aspiring to be a barber, beautician, cosmetologist, or salon owner, learn from my past mistakes and experiences when reading this book. I promise you, if you retain the knowledge in this book and apply it to your profession, you will be successful.

My History of the Barbershop

As far as I can remember, the barbershop has always been a place of congregating, sharing information, debating, fun, and love. Now there is a lot of information out there that will tell you how barbers were surgeons in 1019 BC and how they formed their first organization in France in the 14th century. Listen, I don't know if any of that information is true, so I'm not going to act as if I'm some smart scholar giving you a history lesson. I was born in 1970, I've never been to France, and I don't like to fly. So I'm going to give you the history of the barbershop which is true and meaningful to me.

My mom and dad separated when I was a baby, so my mom provided me with my first visit to the barbershop. I lived with my mom in Kinloch, Missouri. Kinloch was a community in which everything was Black owned. We had our own fire station, police station, high school, shoe stores, candy stores, and of course, a barbershop. I'm older now, and it brings tears to my eyes to think about the love I got from the man who first laid a pair of clippers on my head. His name was Lucious. I can hear his voice now, "Hey, Champeene, hey, Champeene, come on in," as I walked in the door. Now, understand that my nickname was Champ, but this is what he called me, and I loved it. He knew I didn't have my dad around much, and this was one of his many ways to show me love.

Because of the separation between my mom and my dad at such a young age, I didn't have a male figure in my household. It was my mom, my two older sisters, and me. Like any other young boy with no male figure in the household, I was looking for attention from a man. I was looking for security, safety, protection, leadership, empathy, sympathy, and just a man that could teach me about life. Growing up in the hood can be very challenging when you're light skinned, skinny, and scared with no fighting skills and no one to call for back up if you get into a scuffle. There was a steep learning curve for how things are on the streets, and it was not easy for me in the beginning. But when I tell you the words of Lucious got me through many tough times, please believe me.

One day, my mom told me she was taking me to get a haircut, and at the time I didn't realize the impact this would have on my life. I remember hopping into her four-door, white Oldsmobile Ninety-Eight and riding down Monroe Avenue listening to Teddy Pendergrass's "When Somebody Loves You Back." As we arrived at the barbershop, I remember walking to the door wondering if we were going into a house because of the residential screen door on the entrance.

"How y'all doing, how y'all doing?" Lucious said as we entered the door. Lucious didn't stutter, he just repeated exactly what he said at least two or three times.

I was only five years old at the time, and I still remember the name of the first haircut he gave me. My mom told him to cut it low, and then Lucious replied, "Covatis."

Now, Lucious had his own way of doing things. Lucious didn't have a microwave, so he would have a sandwich wrapped in aluminum foil sitting on top of a space heater next to the 20-inch black-and-white television with a hanger as an antenna. When Lucious would take a lunch break, he would grab his toasted sandwich from the space heater and go into a room in the back of the shop. I never saw him eat lunch in front of anyone. From the moment I sat in his chair, a bond and a true friendship for life began. Lucious encouraged me, showed interest in me, and made me feel as if I could do anything, and as I grew up, I became a highly recruited football star. I felt like I wanted to make my mother proud of me, the city of Kinloch proud of me, and Lucious proud of me. When I was scared to fight the neighborhood bullies, Lucious would tell his son Stephon to look out for me. I felt like I had a brother who had my back. But the most amazing thing about Lucious was that he showed love to not only me, but to the entire Kinloch community. Lucious had a way of making you feel as if you were his favorite person in the whole wide world. Every year, when it was time to go back to school, I would hear Lucious telling many of the single-parent mothers who couldn't afford to get their son's hair cut, "Go on now, go on now, I said don't worry about it, don't worry about it now, just pay me when you can." I know very few of those parents paid Lucious the money back.

As the hairstyles changed and the years passed by, my appreciation and love for Lucious grew stronger and stronger. I knew if I needed words of encouragement, words of wisdom, or just a friend to talk to, Lucious would be at the shop telling me to come on in!

I would later go on to play football in college at Northern Illinois University and the University of Memphis and professionally overseas. I kept in contact with Lucious for many years, and I bumped into Stephon, who told me Lucious was doing fine. It's funny how people in our lives show up to get us through a particular moment in time and then go their own way. It makes me sad sometimes to think about how Lucious cared about me and all of the other kids, parents, and people in Kinloch. So, for me, being a barber is more than just removing hair for money. For me, being a barber means you are a good person, a role model, a problem solver, a pillar in the community, and a friend. Lucious, I don't know if I'll ever see you again, but I want you to know I thank God for you being in my life as a kid. I'm thankful for the laughs, the talks, the words of encouragement, and the love you showed my entire Kinloch family. Love you always, Champ, a.k.a. Champeene.

How I Earned My First Million

After my professional football career didn't exactly turn out the way I intended, I found myself back home in my mom's basement. I couldn't believe after all the work I'd done, after all the pain and sacrifice, after all the praying, after all the hill running, after all the holding on and pursuing my dream of playing in the NFL, I was right back where I started. Embarrassment and depression started to take over. I began hanging out all night, drinking, and not really focusing on anything. I can only recall one other time in my life when I felt so much pain: when my mom told me she had breast cancer during my redshirt year at the University of Memphis. I can honestly tell you I was lost, heartbroken, devastated, and angry.

One morning, after I had stayed out all night, my mother came into my room around six in the morning and said, "No man in my house is going to stay out all night and sleep all day! Son, what are you going to do with yourself? You've got to figure something out. Why don't you enroll in barbering school?"

Hearing the disappointment and disgust in my mother's voice made me realize it was time to finally let go of the game I loved and move on to a new chapter in my life. I looked at myself in the mirror and reflected on all the good times and accomplishments I'd experienced in football. I cried and sang the song I use to sing to God when I would jog through the neighborhood; it went like this: "I'm the boy with a dream, I'm the boy with a dream, I got a dream!" I would chant that over and over again every time I trained. I finally accepted that it was over. It was time to move on.

The following morning, I went and enrolled in the International Barbering School in Ferguson, Missouri. After I enrolled, I headed up the street to another place in Ferguson, the University of Missouri–St. Louis, and enrolled to finish the degree I had left unfinished at the University of Memphis. As I started to move around, get active, and get my competitive juices flowing, I started to feel better. I told myself it was time to pick up the pieces and make myself successful. I would not allow myself to turn into a bum and disappoint my mother—or myself. I started talking to myself again to hype myself up, like I had when I played football. I realized that even though I wasn't playing a game or preparing for a season, I needed to approach this new game with the same intensity I played football. I was back! For the first time in a long time, I felt my swag. I was ready and excited to play the game of life! I told myself, *Look, you've been here before, you've been looked over, counted out, doubted, and pushed to the side with your back against the ropes. It's time to strap up your big-boy boots and go take what you want!*

I was focused on a new adventure. I felt like I had a new start at life, a new challenge, a new opportunity. Even if I wasn't going to play in the NFL, I was still going to make NFL money. Therefore, I would implement the same self-discipline, work ethic, focus, sacrifice, and enthusiasm to my education and barbering. It was on like a pot of neck bones!

The work schedule I prepared for myself was relentless and grueling. It was almost as if I was trying to punish myself at times for not actually playing in the NFL. I would get up at seven in the morning, and my day wouldn't end until eleven or twelve at night. I was obsessed with being successful and decided in my mind I wasn't going to lose. My work schedule consisted of four things: barbering school, college, working with my dad, and working out. I would work with my father cutting trees to earn cash while attending school. As the months went by, my confidence increased and my heartbreak from not playing in the NFL started to ease up. My friends and my mother thought I was crazy because of the "no days off" schedule I'd created for myself. It was almost like I was working in a state of fear, now that I think about it. I was actually afraid of not being successful, so I decided to grind nonstop! As the months flew by and I finally passed my barber examination, the opportunity of a lifetime was presented to me.

My mother was having trouble at the barbershop with the barbers working there. The guys working in the barbershop were some good guys, but it's hard sometimes to separate personal feelings from the logistics of business. At the time, my mother wasn't actually cutting hair in the barbershop, and the barbers took advantage of her absence. We all know when the cat's away, the mice will play! There were four barbers working in the shop, and all of them planned on leaving at the same time. My mom was devastated; she was sitting in her room one evening, and this is how the conversation went: "Son, all the barbers at the shop are leaving. I'm thinking about letting the shop go. Do you want to take it over?"

I looked at my mother and said, "I do, Momma, I do, and I promise you I will make it the best barbershop this city has ever seen." I told my mother, "As long as I'm making money, you will be making money." Once again, all, it was on like a pot of neck bones!

So, that night, I couldn't sleep a wink. All I could think about was how I was going to turn this small, four-chair barbershop into a top-notch operation. The first thing I would need was three other barbers who would understand my vision and be able to work at the level I expected. I needed some guys who were hungry for financial success and willing to go the extra mile to get that paper. So I called my best friend from my youth, Marty Robinson. He was pushing shopping carts at Walmart. I told him about the opportunity I had and that I wanted him to come work with me. I knew I could trust him, and I knew we would work well together. I'd known him since kindergarten. But there was one problem: he didn't have a barber license, and he didn't know how to cut a lick of hair. The only time this boy had seen a pair of clippers was when they were being used on his own head.

"Ay, man, listen, I'm taking over the shop, and we can make a lot of money. I need you to come work with me," I said.

"How am I going to work in a barbershop when I don't know how to cut hair, dog?" Marty replied.

"Don't worry about that, man, you can learn to cut at barbering school."

"Barbering school?" Marty replied. "How am I going to get into barbering school?"

"I'm going take you over to the International Barbering School and get you enrolled, that's how." I knew with my best buddy by my side, there was no stopping us. When Marty started barbering school, I would go up there to check on him from time to time. I had previously graduated from barbering school, and a guy I was in school with was soon to be graduating as well; his name was Martez Stephenson. Martez was a smooth operator, a hustler, a go-getter, and a ladies' man. Martez had what I like to call swag, but most of all, Martez was a good dude who wanted to be successful in life. I told Martez about my barbershop, and I asked him to come join Marty and me. Martez and I had the same perspective when it came to working hard and wanting more. We saw things the same way and ended up becoming friends.

I had two barbers coming, and I only needed one more. One day, I was cleaning up the barbershop and a guy stopped by inquiring about a job. He walked into the shop as I was taking the trash out and said, "How you doing? I was wondering if you had any booths available?" I stood there for a moment in silence; I couldn't believe this was happening so soon. "I was wondering if you had any booths available," he repeated.

I didn't want to sound too eager; I had to act as if I had plenty of people trying to work with me. "How long you been cutting?" I replied.

"I've been cutting three years, and I'm looking for a new place to cut," he said.

"Well, you just found it," I replied. He said his name was Dre. We sat and talked for hours, and he possessed the qualities I was looking for. And there you have it, ladies and gentlemen, the new Cut Styles and More: me, Marty, Martez, and Dre.

If I told you I was as hungry as a pit bull gnawing on a chicken bone for success, that would be an understatement. As my new team joined me at the shop, I implemented a standard of excellence and out-worked the competition in the area. We walked the streets handing out flyers. I donated pencils to the local school district with the name of the shop on them. We created customer call lists. We gave away free donuts on Saturday mornings. We kept the shop super clean. We played good music. We laughed. We had a Soul Train line that allowed the customers to do their favorite dance moves. We encouraged one another. We shared with one another. We cared. And we made a lot of money! All four of us purchased new cars, and for the first time in a long time, I felt good about my work. I was a part of a different kind of team—not a team where I was running touchdowns or catching passes, but a team where I was doing linings and bald fades.

I was making so much money I ended up purchasing the building where I was renting my space. The landlord and owner, Mr. Mertz, was a very kind man, and I know he saw something in me that he liked. Mr. Mertz sold me the entire strip mall for only about $250,000. The building appraised for a lot more than that—I can't tell you everything! So here I was, owning my own barbershop and strip mall, which led to me grossing my first million dollars. I ended up knocking a wall down in the building and expanding Cut Styles and More into a 20-chair barber and beauty salon. I would eventually sell the entire building for close to a million dollars and move locations years later. I still own Cut Styles and More. What one man can do, you can do.

Understanding the
Boss Mentality

Unlike any other country on this planet, the United States of America has set a standard across the world for the true meaning of freedom and economic growth. There is no other land in the world that has produced more rags-to-riches stories quite like America has. Many foreigners and immigrants dream of coming to America to provide their families a better way of life financially, socially, and emotionally. Let's face it, there's no place in the world that's had more success stories of people going from living in poverty to living in luxury. The opportunities for success, the opportunities for wealth, and the opportunities to be a boss in America are endless. But, as you should know, just because the opportunity is given doesn't mean the road to financial prosperity is easy in our country. In order to live the true American financial dream, one must understand the meaning of a boss mentality and incorporate this psychological logic into their financial journey.

What is a boss? A boss is a go-getter, a hustler, a visionary, and a leader of people. A boss recognizes the opportunity for financial gain and is able to formulate strategies to monetize their efforts. A boss understands the importance of time and recognizes the cost of each and every second of the day. When conducting business throughout the day, a boss can't afford to waste time on meaningless conversation or activities not conducive to financial gain. A boss is always aware of time and moves with a sense of urgency throughout the workday.

A boss understands the power of research and education as it pertains to their business and wants to know everything about it. A boss realizes if they don't become a master of every detail relatable to their business, they run the risk of being taking advantage of and cheated. A boss knows when, where, and why their money is being allocated and accepts nothing less than what they have paid for. A boss is firm, direct, and able to remove personal emotion from the equation when doing business. A boss must always do business from a logical standpoint and not allow other people's emotions to derail them from the objective of doing business: to GET MONEY!

A boss does not procrastinate or make reasons or excuses for a lack of production. A boss is a problem solver and approaches all problems when doing business with a direct solution. A boss doesn't have time to deflect solutions to a problem; they are always direct and to the point when faced with a challenge. A boss understands that when people don't answer questions directly, it usually means they're not being honest or they're trying to shift the narrative of the conversation to something that could deflect from the issue at hand. A boss understands the importance of separating business from personal and will not allow anyone to manipulate their philosophy. A boss understands that in business most people aren't loyal to them personally, and that people are only interested in what they can get.

A boss invests their own money and is a risk taker, motivator, innovator, and leader who understands the importance of economic growth. A boss is proactive and reactive when implementing solutions to challenges that occur when operating a business. A boss's primary objective when doing business is to make money. A boss understands that if they don't implement the psychology and practices of being a boss, they will soon be out of business.

My question to you: Are you ready to be a boss?

Being a boss can be challenging, and if you aren't ready to be a boss just yet, review these principles I have given you and use them to your advantage. I've been the boss of many companies, and I would advise you to stick to these principles when opening your business. People will challenge your vision, principles, and morals, but you must stick to what you believe in and stay committed to your objective.

Stop Being Tricked

What if I told you there was a job paying $70 an hour? What if I told you there was a job paying $70 an hour that provided benefits, health insurance, retirement, and vacation time? What if I told you that you already had the job, and the only thing you had to do was show up? Most people would yell, scream, and holler about their new job. They would be so happy to have a job that paid so well. Well, I have some good news for you!

To my fellow barbers and beauticians: If you possess hair-styling skills, customer service skills, and a strong desire to be successful, you have the job! Congratulations, you have just hired yourself! That's right, what were you thinking? Oh, I get it, you were probably thinking some other company was going to hire you. Ladies and gentlemen, I'm about to redirect your mindset and get you to realize the power and greatness you have in you. As a barber or beautician, it's time for us to stop disrespecting our trade and embrace the greatness we have in our own hands. If you took time out of your life to learn a skill, if you sacrificed family time and relationships, if you spent money, if you obtained a license to be a hair stylist or barber, you deserve to get paid! The only person that can stop you from generating the amount of income you want is YOU! This chapter of the book isn't for the weak, the insecure, the shy, or the non-believer; this chapter is strictly for the dreamers and goal-reachers who understand it's possible.

The problem with most entrepreneurs who never reach their intended objective is simple: their minds aren't in a place of self-belief. As cliché as this may sound, it's true. You see, most people find it easier and safer to believe in someone else instead of themselves. These non-self-believers are afraid to take on any challenges that could possibly result in them feeling pain or losing resources. These non-self-believers find comfort in playing it safe and acting as if they're the boss or in charge of something. Along with being lazy, fearful, and weak, these non-self-believers usually like to gossip and complain about other people's accomplishments and creations. These non-self-believers usually hide behind a title or a name tag that another person stamped them with and act as if they've got it going on. They're quick to judge, quick to critique, quick to doubt, quick to make excuses, quick to give up, and quick to tell other people what they should and shouldn't be doing. As bosses, our mindset is totally the opposite of non-self-believers. Let me explain.

First of all, let me make one thing clear: not everyone can be a boss! If you enjoy being told what to do, when to take a lunch break, when to go to the bathroom, how long to stay, when to take a vacation, when to wear jeans, when to use your cell phone, or when to stand up or sit down, I'm not talking to you; please close the book and go read your employee manual, because this book isn't for you. A true boss is uncomfortable in a setting in which they're being told what to do. It actually makes them angry when someone is barking out instructions, duties, and obligations they don't feel passionate about. A true boss understands the ability they have in themselves and is willing to take the risks associated with achieving their goals. A true boss is unhappy and miserable if they aren't pursuing what inspires them and what they're passionate about. The mindset of a true boss is "I will not stop until I win!" My purpose in writing this book was to get all of my fellow boss barbers and beauticians to realize the power is in our hands.

The problem with most people who never reach their goal in life is that they can't handle being uncomfortable. They have developed a thought process that tells them they should avoid being uncomfortable. They find comfort in knowing someone else has taken on the risk of owning a business and has all the responsibility, does all the work, pays them a certain amount of money every two weeks, and promises them a retirement check in 30 years. So these people spend the prime of their lives chasing a retirement check, and when they're old and gray, find themselves wishing they would have done something different. Do you know anyone like that? Of course you do!

Listen to me: You don't need someone to give you a name tag, dictate to you, control you, intimidate you, manipulate you, promise you a retirement, and act as if you're beneath them to make money. You have the power right in your hands to be a boss and control your own financial future. You can give yourself a paycheck, you can give yourself health-care benefits, you can set yourself up for retirement, and you can live the life you want to live with your clippers and shears. With the right mindset and perspective on life, you don't have to get pushed around at some deadbeat job by corny people anymore. Here are some of my beliefs and information that support the boss mentality. Pay attention!

1. How to establish benefits as a barber or beautician

Many barbers and beauticians have departed from the hair industry simply because they have been tricked into believing they can't obtain their own health benefits, insurance, and retirement. Listen, there is a ton of information on the internet on obtaining health insurance and benefits for the self-employed. You can simply Google "how to get health insurance and benefits if I'm self-employed," and you will find the information you need. It's that easy. Stop allowing these employers to trick you into thinking you have to work for someone in order to receive benefits, health insurance, and a retirement check. It's not true! The employers also have to contact a benefit-providing agency that provides their employees with the exact same coverages you can get for yourself. Instead, you do the research, you educate yourself, and you make the call. Stop putting your livelihood in someone else's hands. You can do for yourself the same thing they're doing for you. Discipline yourself and don't be lazy if you want to reach your financial and life goals. Becoming a barber or beautician doesn't have to mean you live without the proper medical and retirement benefits. There are so many options and companies out there waiting on your call. I'll suggest one: call the National Association for the Self-Employed (NASE). They are a good place to start your search.

2. Self-discipline

Most people can't flourish as entrepreneurs because they lack self-discipline. These people lack the ability to focus their energy and efforts on the objective they're trying to achieve. They would rather spend their time on activities not conducive to their life's purposes and missions like watching television, sleeping excessively, partying, vacationing, small talk, going to movies, and wasting time. When you fully embrace the boss mentality, you will understand the importance of self-discipline and realize that your success depends on it. My fellow barbers and beauticians: I've made it my business to give you the necessary business skills in order for you to reach your financial goals and dreams. Take pride in what you do. Stop sitting around complaining about someone else's job when you have the ability to create your own. It makes my stomach hurt to see so many barbers and beauticians abandoning their talents because of the lack of entrepreneurial education and self-discipline. There's power in the clippers and shears; all you have to do is become a master of research and a student of the game. Stand up and fight for your financial freedom!

3. Discard laziness

The problem with a lot of my barbers and beauticians is they're simply lazy. They don't want to do the work it takes to be a successful entrepreneur and boss. They would rather make someone else rich and be told what to do instead of doing what it takes to fill their desires. Most people want to be successful, but they also don't want to do the work and go through the pain it takes to be successful. For example, I hear people say things like, "I don't like expensive cars, they're a waste of money." So you mean to tell me if someone gave you a Lamborghini, you wouldn't like it? Or is it that you're not willing to do the work it takes to afford a Lamborghini, so you tell yourself you don't like expensive cars? What I'm trying to tell you is this: In order for you to get what you want out of this life, you're going to go through some pain, setbacks, sacrifice, loneliness, confusion, frustration, and more! But trust me when I tell you that the top is so much better than the bottom. Get up off your gluteus maximus and make it happen!

4. Stay consistent

As a barber or beautician, you must understand the importance of consistency as it pertains to being a boss. When you're marketing your goods and services, you must be able to produce a product of value. A haircut, a conditioner, a tool, a service—it doesn't matter what the product is, but it does matter if the product is consistently amazing. When you're able to sustain consistency in the marketplace, you will begin to develop repeat customers, and this is what you want. You want customers to repeatedly purchase your goods and services day after day, week after week, month after month, and year after year. The repetitive customer base will allow you to stabilize a financial foundation while working toward growing your profit margins. Each and every day, you must ensure you're utilizing every resource available to assist you in establishing a repeat clientele.

5. The power of research

Ever since internet search engines began to index the internet in the early '90s, the internet's information has been available for nearly everyone to access. The days of not being able to find the information you need to own a business are over. As a boss, you must be able to research information that pertains to the operation of your business at any time. The internet will allow you to research any information you choose. There is no reason for anyone in today's world to be ignorant. The power of research and information is right at our fingertips. All you have to do is literally Google whatever you want to know, and the answers to your questions will appear like magic. Stop playing with your life and Google the information you need to know in order to live out your dreams.

Committing to the Grind

hear people talking in the barbershop all day every day about what they have done, what they are doing, and what they will be doing in the future. And what I've come to realize is that most people are doing just that, simply talking. Having a dream or a goal is a beautiful thing to have, but living that dream or reaching that goal is a grind!

The thing I want you to understand about pursuing a dream or reaching a goal is that discomfort and pain will show up to test your will to win. If you don't have the mental strength to hammer through adverse conditions, you will be like everyone else talking in the barbershop: average! These talkers don't have the will to be anything but average, and they are okay with that. The talkers only enjoy talking about being successful, because they never have to feel the mental and physical discomfort that comes with being great. The talkers spend hours of their time praising the accomplishments of others while precious seconds of their own lives are ticking away. The talkers have figured out that they're not tough enough to do anything above average because of their pain tolerance. Talkers hide behind the achievements of others as if they have completed those particular tasks. In the world of sports, many fans are talkers. There's nothing wrong with being a fan if that's what you choose to be.

But you have to ask yourself: *What have I done to cheer about in my own life?* and *What will I do significantly enough that someone will want to be a fan of mine?*

Listen: Don't be a talker. Don't be afraid to discipline yourself and go after what you want in this life. The only thing that can stop you from getting what you want is you! Go after your hopes and dreams, and commit to the grind!

Becoming a
Master Barber or Beautician

In order to become a master barber or beautician, you must first understand the physical and psychological commitment you will need to reach mastery. The educational process in your pursuit to mastery will be the foundation of your journey. Therefore, you will have to discipline yourself to read, study, and research the information necessary to become a master.

You will need to find a barber or cosmetology school that offers licensure in your particular field of choice. There are many technical training/trade schools across the country that offer barber and cosmetology training, but you will need to research the quality of each school to see if their curriculum will truly assist you in reaching your goal of mastery. Just like any other business, some schools are awful and simply take advantage of students trying to pursue their hopes of becoming a master barber or beautician.

When selecting a barber or cosmetology school, you must ensure they will give you all the tools necessary to monetizing your trade. The school should teach you the skill set to perform all hair and body services. You must also understand that each state requires certification. You must pass practical and written exams to be licensed in cosmetology, so don't waste time at an institution where the instruction isn't conducive to your goal. Some schools will literally not teach you anything. I've seen situations where instructors gave students books, sat them in a classroom, and took an eight-hour coffee break. That's why it's important to have a conversation with the owner to inform them of your purpose of attending before selecting a barber or cosmetology school. You want to let them know how serious you are about your career and that you will not accept being mistreated or cheated out of your opportunity. You don't want to be stuck in some classroom with a textbook all day, expected to teach yourself while the instructor smokes cigarettes, talks on the phone, and eats donuts. Tell the owner you want to be given an educational opportunity in which you can receive data-based instruction from an experienced instructor.

An excellent barber or cosmetology school should teach you all of the skills needed for you to be able to be successful in your career. Be on the lookout for these key essential factors when selecting a barber or cosmetology school:

- **Course curriculum**. The cosmetology school that's the best for you will offer everything needed for you to be successful in your career. It will provide you with the skill training needed to reach mastery. That could mean hair coloring, clipper cutting, shear cutting, and more. Select a school you feel will meet your needs and is able to differentiate instruction.

- **Practical business skills.** If your goal is to be a barbershop or beauty shop boss, you'll need to have impeccable business skills. A top barber or cosmetology school will offer business training in their curriculum in order to provide all students with the knowledge it takes to be a successful business owner in the marketplace.

- **Exam preparation.** You must ensure the institution of your choice is dedicated to helping you pass the state-mandated exam, allowing you to become a licensed barber or beautician.

- **Industry involvement.** Who are the instructors? How much experience do they have in the profession? Do they attend professional development opportunities to improve their knowledge and skill set in the industry? What valuable tips and tricks can they show you to help you be the best barber or cosmetologist you can be? These are questions you need to ask yourself, the administration, and the owner of the institution you select.

- **Hands-on student salon.** This is a key component in deciding which school to choose. In order to develop and improve as a barber or cosmetologist, you must be able to practice. If a school can't give you the repetitions needed to enhance your performance, look for a different school. You want to make certain you can practice what you will learn on real clients in a real salon setting. Plastic dummies don't talk, move, or complain the way a real person will once you're in the workplace. A real salon setting will give you a hands-on experience in preparing you for your career.

- **Visit**. I highly recommend you visit more than one school to get a feel for the learning environment and culture of each school. Interview the staff, administration, and owners to ensure they are going to provide you with the education needed to reach your goals. Talk to current students or graduates to see if they were happy with their choice of school and if they felt the curriculum lacked anything essential. Take your career seriously, and don't allow people to intimidate you when asking questions, giving answers, and looking for a school suitable for you. GO GET IT!

If you are going to become successful in barbering and/or cosmetology, you must be able to sacrifice the time it's going to take to achieve that goal. You must discipline yourself and focus on mastering all of the mechanical, technical, and business-related factors pertaining to barbering and cosmetology. This will not be an easy task, and problems will occur in your quest to reach mastery. However, if you can push through the challenges and stay focused on the objective, you will reach your goal. YOU CAN DO IT!

What to Watch Out for as a Barbershop or Beauty Shop Owner

The shop can be one of the most entertaining, fun, and exciting work environments a person could ever dream of working in. For a shop to operate smoothly, the culture of the barbershop or beauty shop must be in line with the professional expectations of the owner, and all of the employees must buy into the philosophy of success. But we all know there are many challenges that come with trying to get a group of individuals to work together cohesively. As a boss, one of your biggest challenges will be maintaining a professional, peaceful, organized, and clean work environment for your staff and customers. You need to understand that it's human nature to challenge authority, and trust me when I tell you: You will be challenged! This chapter will lay out all of the many challenges I've faced throughout my years of owning and working in a barbershop. Also, I want all of my beauticians who plan on opening their own shops to know they will most likely be faced with the exact same challenges. Here are the red flags to watch out for:

1. Bad attitudes

One of the most frustrating things as a shop owner is dealing with an employee or independent contractor with a bad attitude. I don't understand the mindset of people who act as if someone owes them something or that they're better than everyone else. Where do they get this sense of entitlement? One minute they're chatty and friendly, the next they're unfriendly and not talking—I can't keep up! My advice to you is simple: Get rid of them immediately! Trust me when I tell you that they mean you and your business no good. These people are like a cancer that needs to be removed in order to keep living. I know what you're thinking. You're thinking you need the booth rent money or the commission income from them. Listen to me: You don't need cancer! Answer this question: How much would you charge to keep cancer in your body? That sounds ridiculous doesn't it? In the long and short run, a person with a bad attitude will destroy your business and your happiness. Don't allow anyone to destroy your business or your happiness. Fight through the financial setback until you find a better replacement!

2. Lazy stylists

Some people are just flat-out lazy, and in a world that's continuously moving and advancing, there is no place for laziness. The lazy stylist will come into the shop and sit down immediately without checking to see if anything needs to be done. The lazy stylist will leave messes wherever they go—their work area, their tools and equipment, the break room, the bathroom—and they will only do the bare minimum to get by. As a boss, you need to communicate to the lazy stylist the importance of teamwork and sanitation when trying to earn revenue. Let the lazy stylist know they should check to see what can be done to improve the condition of the shop whenever they come in. You should have shop-cleaning rules and expectations of the culture of the shop in a handbook in order to eliminate any confusion of your expectations. Stay on top of your game. Don't accept mediocre effort when it comes to your business. If your business is your livelihood, why would you allow someone to disrespect what feeds you and your family? Let the lazy stylist know they can no longer be lazy if they want to continue earning money with you.

3. Disrespectful clients

Some people are flat-out disrespectful, and as a boss, you will continuously have to let disrespectful clients know how to conduct themselves in your place of business. As a child, I had to learn that people do to you what you allow them to do to you. In other words, you teach people how to treat you. When clients come into your place of business using profanity, intoxicated, high, smelling like weed, yelling, putting their feet on your furniture, or allowing their kids to be out of control, you, as a boss, must politely inform them of their behaviors and how those behaviors will not be tolerated. You're the one who took the risk of opening up your own shop, you're the one who is responsible for your shop, and you're the one who sacrificed time and money to start your own business. These disrespectful people care about you or your sacrifices, and it's your responsibility to care about your own stuff. Don't, don't, *don't* allow them to disrespect your establishment. Put them in their place! Here's what you say to them: "Please control your children; please get your feet off my furniture; please stop talking so loud; please don't come in here drunk or high or smelling like weed—*please!*"

4. Solicitors and boosters

The barbershop or beauty shop has always been the heartbeat of the community. In the shop you can hear any subject being debated. The barbershop has always been an informational hub— a place where businessmen met and discussed trending topics, families gathered to receive services, and people came to simply hang out. So what better place for a solicitor or booster to find potential buyers? As a boss, I highly recommend you don't allow solicitors or boosters to use your business as a place to sell their goods. First of all, if you're leasing or renting a space, you have to pay a monthly fee in order to make money. So why would you allow someone to walk into your business and make money for free? It doesn't make sense! You are in business to monetize your goods and services, not someone else's. If you have to pay someone to make money, then the boosters and solicitors need to find a place to lease or rent and sell their products. Look at it this way: Do you think McDonald's would allow you to come into their restaurant and set up a barber chair and perform haircuts on your clients? Of course not. In order for others to respect your business, you must respect your business. Nobody makes money for free! Also, how do you know the products being sold are any good and not stolen? As a boss, you must always protect your business, and if a booster is selling stolen goods out of your shop, you could possibly find yourself in legal trouble. I don't want you to get into legal trouble, so please, no soliciting.

5. Gambling in the shop

Ever since I can remember, the barbershop has always been the place where men debated, argued, yelled, and screamed about their favorite sports teams and players. The level of analyzation on the stats of theses sports teams by some of these customers has been truly impressive over the years. A friendly disagreement of opinion on a particular matter can easily turn into a small wager. As a boss, I recommend you don't allow customers, independent contractors, or employees to gamble or bet in your shop. I don't care how small or large the amount of money is; you don't want to be responsible for any turmoil when someone doesn't pay. Disagreements over money can easily escalate into a serious matter. Also, you don't want your business to be known as somewhere you can place a bet. That reputation could possibly lead you into legal trouble. Do yourself a favor: Don't allow any form of gambling in your business.

6. Unprofessional tenants

If you are leasing or renting a storefront, a space in a strip mall, or a building where there are other tenants, your business could be affected by the practices of other tenants. For instance, my barbershop is located in a strip mall where I'm in between a cell phone company and a Chinese restaurant. For years, I've been doing business in this particular strip mall without any plumbing issues or problems. My barbershop has been in the same place since before the Chinese restaurant and cell phone company arrived. All of a sudden, one day, my toilet backed up and filled with grease—hmm, I wonder where that came from? You guessed it, the Chinese restaurant grease somehow backed up the lines connecting to my barbershop, according to the plumbing service I hired. This could have been caused by the restaurant not properly cleaning their grease trap. When I saw my toilet filled with grease, I immediately went to ask the manger next door if they were aware of a backup or flooding. The point I'm trying to make is this: Because of the actions (or inactions) of the Chinese restaurant, I had to call a plumbing company to handle the situation. The business practices of my neighboring tenant caused me a lot of frustration and extra work. As a boss, you want to be able to speak with neighboring tenants in a respectful manner when trying to resolve any misunderstandings, accidents, or mistakes. Always be clear and direct with all tenants in your building, and make sure you are following all of the rules of your lease agreement. You can't control what other people do, but you can control what you do.

7. Workers who don't follow sanitation rules

As a boss, you must understand that you're responsible for everything that happens in your business. You will have people who simply don't like to follow rules. They will give you every reason in the book for doing the wrong thing. What you must understand is that these people don't care about your business; the only thing they care about is what they can get from your business. Do not allow anyone working in your establishment to avoid following rules and regulations. Your governing State Board of Cosmetology and Barber Examiners implements their sanitation rules in order to protect the public, customers, and stylists. People make mistakes and accidents occur, but to intentionally violate the regulations is rude and disrespectful. You're the boss for a reason, and it's your responsibility to correct or discipline anyone who jeopardizes your operation.

8. Slumlords

When I sit and think about the many challenges that come with doing business, the primary challenge for any businessperson is always boils down to getting people to do what they are supposed to do. This appears to be the most common problem—not only professionally, but also personally. Imagine if everyone simply did what they were supposed to do; this world would definitely be a better place. But that's not reality, and that's why we have to hold people accountable for their actions. Make sure you read and understand all of the responsibilities of the landlord or property management company in your lease. One of the biggest mistakes small business owners make is not reading and understanding documents they sign. Before putting your signature on anything, ensure you understand what you're signing. Particularly if there is anything confusing in a contract, you should have an attorney review it with you to point out any potential problems.In business, trust is substituted by contracts and legally binding agreements for a reason. As a boss, you must operate from a position of logic and discard trust and emotion. Trust will have you out of business, bankrupt, homeless, and wondering what happened! Highlight the duties and responsibilities of your land-lord and follow the procedures of the lease when there is an issue.

9. Borrowers

It's one thing to need a favor from time to time, but it's another thing to beg others simply because you're too lazy to handle your responsibility. In my barbershop, I worked with a particular barber who never had what he needed to work with. Every other day, he wanted to bor-row this or that, and after a while, I got sick of it. Listen to me: Some people are looking for someone to scam, beat, and cheat to get whatever they can for themselves. These dirtbags only care about themselves. Their game is to hustle anything and everything they can for their own personal gain. That has to be a miserable life! These people are usually lazy, jealous, selfish, disloyal, untrustworthy, and greedy. They walk around pretending to be something they're not because of their low self-esteem and lack of character. Hold people accountable for their own actions, and teach your stylists to maintain professionalism at all times. Purchasing the proper tools and supplies is a huge part of barbering and cosmetology. If a lazy stylist doesn't commit to preparing themselves for the workday, I've learned to teach them to prepare themselves by not giving them anything. Why should I continue to give a person something when they're lazy? Don't do it. Make them get their own stuff!

10. Misbehaved children

Listen, you didn't invest money and time into opening a barbershop or beauty salon for some kids to come in and destroy it. It's amazing to me how parents sit there and watch their children walk on furniture, yell, run, leave crumbs everywhere, and urinate on the bathroom floor. Really! I don't blame the children for the inappropriate behavior. I blame the parents. Children are young and still learning, but grown folks need to teach their children how to behave in a public setting. You can't allow them to demonstrate disruptive behavior in your shop. In a situation when the child is not behaving well, first ask the parent to please control their child. If they can't seem to get their child under control, you should ask them to leave. You can't allow one customer to negatively affect 20 customers. All behavior is learned; children do what they are allowed and taught to do. Don't allow a child to destroy your business.

11. Customer poachers

One of the tricky things about barbers and beauticians paying booth rent is drawing the line when spending promotional dollars on increasing the shop's clientele. I've experienced barbers sitting back and benefitting from my hard promotional work and dollars without spending one cent on promoting themselves. These types of people are takers, and their only concern is getting as many customers as possible without having to spend any money or do any work. They will sit back and collect phone numbers from customers they didn't even bring into the shop. But as a boss, you must understand their mentality and continue to promote your business.

Many times, barbershop and beauty shop owners don't understand the difference between an employee and an independent contractor. Let me explain: When a stylist pays you to rent a booth, they are not your employee. When a person is considered an employee of yours, you have to cut them a check in which federal, state, and local taxes are deducted. You will have to carry workers' compensation insurance, and in some instances, provide health-care benefits. There is way more responsibility when a person is employed by you directly.

On the other hand, a barber or beautician that pays booth rent is considered an independent contractor. When you hire a barber or beautician as an independent contractor, they are responsible for their own health care and benefits, not you. They control when they come to work, when they leave work, the pricing of their services, and the selection of tools they work with. An independent contractor is basically operating as a business within your business. Make sure they obtain a booth rental license if needed in your state. Check with your governing state board to see what the requirements are for independent contractor licensing.

Still want to be a boss? Listen: It's not easy. You will be challenged every day in some shape, form, or fashion. Stay ready for people who will try to destroy your business little by little.

The Power of Research

What does it mean to research? Research is the systematic investigation of materials and sources to establish facts and reach conclusions. Before starting any new business adventure, you must conduct thorough research on the industry you're entering into. In my own adventures, I repeatedly made the mistake of not becoming a student of the game first. I would often find myself being inspired about a particular business venture but didn't take the time needed to conduct thoroughly research the logistics and what it would take to monetize my efforts. I didn't realize starting a business strictly off of inspiration and emotion was not enough. In fact, because of my start-quick, in-a-hurry approach to a new business, I found myself filing for bankruptcy on more than one occasion. I don't want you to go through what I went through financially and emotionally, so please take the information I'm giving to you and use it to your advantage. It's not fun going from a millionaire to having three dollars in your pocket! Also, please understand: Just because research is conducted, it doesn't guarantee you economic success. You can do all of the research in the world and still lose money. It's just a harsh reality of business. Sometimes things go wrong.

By conducting a thorough research process, you'll give yourself a higher percentage of being successful in your particular field of choice. By not conducting a thorough research process, your chances of becoming successful in the business you choose is not likely. Research serves as the foundation of your business and will allow you to remain in a proactive state of mind when developing, growing, and maintaining your business. I'm going to give you seven reasons why research is important. Research is:

1. A tool for building knowledge and for facilitating learning
2. A means to understand various issues and increase public awareness
3. An aid to business success
4. A way to uncover lies and support truths
5. A means to find, gauge, and seize opportunities
6. A seed to love reading, writing, analyzing, and sharing valuable information
7. Nourishment and exercise for the mind

You would be surprised at the number of entrepreneurs who start businesses each year without conducting thorough research. The reason why most people don't research is simply because they're lazy! It's plain and simple: They don't want to do the work it takes to discover all of the possible pitfalls that can hurt their businesses and all the possibilities that could help their businesses. In my opinion, conducting research is a requirement for all business owners in the world. Research serves as the key tool for gaining wisdom and facilitating learning conducive to economic growth. When you are an entrepreneur funding his or her own business from the start, you can't afford to lose revenue because the research process wasn't conducted appropriately. The objective in business is to sell a product or provide a service for economic gain. In other words, TO MAKE MONEY! By not aggressively conducting thorough research, I can almost promise you that, sooner than later, you will pay for the laziness in some shape, form, or fashion. In order to have the best opportunity to increase your margins, you must conduct a thorough investigation of everything that pertains to your business.

Being a boss is a lot of responsibility and hard work, but it's worth it! It's not hard to gain information, form a checklist, and get things done. I would advise you to create a business plan in which you lay out all of the potential expenses you may occur. Once you have a clear vision of what needs to be done, you can then formulate a plan of attack and GET IT DONE. For example, in my barbershop, these are some of my monthly expenses:

1. Cable
2. Electricity
3. Insurance coverage
4. Lease payment
5. Alarm system
6. Phone
7. Window cleaning service
8. Cleaning supplies
9. Internet

As you can see, there are costs involved with making money. That's just the way it goes!

The Importance of
State Board Regulations

One of the biggest things I've learned in business has been the importance of following rules. This chapter will be very short and to the point for two reasons: it doesn't take many words to say "don't break the law and don't put people at risk," and "the laws will be different for each state (and possibly city), so you'll need to do some research on your local governing laws." As a boss, you must realize, every day you wake up, you're going to have to protect your business. You will be tested, you will be tried, and you will have to put people in their place when it comes to following rules. People aren't loyal to you in business; people are only loyal to what your business can provide for them. As soon as they can't get what they need from your business, they will be gone like the wind. So never let anyone avoid the State Board regulations and policies.

Your governing State Board has implemented rules and policies for a reason. I would suggest each and every person working in your barbershop or beauty shop know every State Board rule and policy. Remember this: You're the boss. Don't let someone else's lack of wanting to read take you out of business. As bosses, we must know the rules of the game we're playing! Complying with State

Board regulations for barbering and cosmetology in your state is not hard at all. The requirements in each state are different, and you can find your state's specific requirements on their website or by calling and asking for a copy. You must apply yourself and do whatever it takes if you want to be a successful barber or beautician. Here are a few of the requirements you will have to meet as a shop owner:

1. Barber or cosmetologist license
2. Completed barbershop or beauty shop application
3. Lease agreement showing you have a place of business
4. City or county (and/or state) business license
5. Floor plan of salon
6. Properly operating bathrooms
7. Dry cabinets for towel storage
8. Trash cans with liners and lids
9. Container with lid for dirty towels
10. One shampoo bowl per three stylists
11. Hot and cold running water
12. Proper spacing between barber or beauty stations
13. First aid kit

Your state, city, or county may have different requirements for barber or beauty shops to meet, so you should be sure to research what's necessary in your specific instance.

How to Obtain Your Business License When Starting a New Business

When opening a new business, you will need a license in the municipality you choose. Rules and regulations are different in every municipality, so it's important to understand the licensing rules where your barbershop or beauty shop will be located. As a boss, you must operate your business in compliance with the licensing rules. Failure to do so could lead to serious consequences. Understand that a business license registers your business as separate from your personal affairs, and if done correctly, this can give you some legal benefits. So be sure you understand all of the rules and regulations before you even settle on a location. I'm going to give you eight steps to take in order to acquire your business license.

1. Pick your location.

Find a location where you feel your shop will be the most profitable. Choosing a location for your business will be the most important decision you will make in the process of starting your barbershop or beauty salon. The location of your shop will have a direct impact on the amount of money you make. If your location is in an area where there is not much public traffic, you will have a hard time acquiringwalk-in clientele. Find a spot where there is as much curb appeal as possible, where there will be a lot of cars driving by. You want the public and potential clients to have a clear view of where you are. Also, if possible, try to find an area where you are the only provider of that particular service. Now, I'm not telling you to shy away from competition, because after reading this book, you will be able to be successful even if you open up a shop on Pluto. But if we can make it easier on ourselves, why not? Starting a business where there is less competition will increase your chances of attracting customers.

The location of your business will also have a direct impact on the total cost of operation and the amount of taxes you pay. Understand that the more prominent the area, the more expensive it will be to open up shop. Leasing a storefront in a shopping mall or another expensive location will be very costly in the beginning. I recommend that you find a location that meets your budget and take the time to grow your business before moving into an expensive area you can't afford. Remember, the key to business is sustainability and consistency, and in order to be consistent, you must be able to sustain being open!

2. Pick your business name.

You have to decide what you want your name to be. I'm a firm believer that the name of a business can impact sales in a good or bad way. Choosing the right business name is very important, because all of your legal matters will be centered around the name you have chosen. The name you choose will be the center point of your brand. Signs, business cards, flyers, merchandise, advertisements, and marketing materials will all promote your business name. This will be the name the public will associate with the goods and services you provide. Remember this when selecting a business name: A business name has the power of influence and can stir up emotions. Some people may view a name as offensive or distasteful; others may view the same name as amazing and classy. Select a name that represents what you're willing to stand behind and fight for. There is no way to please everyone, but you need to take your time and really think about the name you want representing your brand. Ideally, you'll want to get feedback from your target market on your name before you settle on one. Ask your friends, family, neighbors, local business owners, and others in your community what they think of your potential name(s). You may get conflicting feedback, but if you ask for enough opinions, you may start to see that a majority likes (or dislikes) a name, and then you can make a decision accordingly.

Ideally, you'll want to get feedback from your target market on your name before you settle on one. Ask your friends, family, neighbors, local business owners, and others in your community what they think of your potential name(s). You may get conflicting feedback, but if you ask for enough opinions, you may start to see that a majority likes (or dislikes) a name, and then you can make a decision accordingly.

Finally, you'll want to research that there isn't already a business with the same or similar name in your state or city. Check both Google and your state's licensing office. In addition to not being able to choose an exact business name that's already in use in your state, you'll face difficulty building up name recognition and search engine optimization (SEO) if your name is too close to another business's.

3. Register your business name.

Once you have selected a name for your business, now it's time to ensure you can use that business name. Even if you have an idea of the name you want for your business but you're really not 100% sure, go ahead and register the name so you don't lose it to someone else. You can switch the name later if you choose to do so, but at least you'll have the name in your possession if you want to keep it. When you've made the final decision on your business name, register your business as a limited liability company (LLC).

Understanding how to form an LLC and how it works for your business will give you a financial advantage moving forward in your operation. Most small business owners prefer to operate under an LLC because of the liability protection, management flexibility, and tax advantages you receive once you register your business. Limited liability companies are very popular among small business owners. In my opinion, the biggest advantages of forming an LLC are as follows:

1. Limited personal liability

If your business is a sole proprietorship or a partnership, you must realize that you and your business are the same "person," legally speaking. All of your business expenses are also your expenses personally. Any negligence caused by your partner or anyone in your business could have an effect on your personal assets. An LLC has strict limits on your personal liability because an LLC is separate from its owners by law. An LLC is responsible for its own debts, and any amount of money owed by the LLC is owed by the LLC—you can't be sued personally to relieve that debt owed by the LLC. Personal assets like your car, house, boat, bank account, and favorite pair of blue jeans can't be used to pay off business debt. Your personal assets are always protected.

2. Convenience/less paperwork

For a small business like a barbershop or beauty shop, it's generally unnecessary to form a corporation and deal with all of the red tape that comes along with that, like holding annual shareholding meetings, publishing annual reports, paying annual fees to the state, and a lot of record keeping. With an LLC, you don't have to bother with all of the maintenance it takes to have a corporation. You can simply register your LLC within the state you're in, write an operating agreement (standard operating agreements can be found online), and you're done. In most states, LLCs don't need to file annual reports.

3. Taxes

When you are the owner of an LLC, the LLC's income and expenses can be filed on your personal tax return. You, as the owner, will pay personal income tax on any profits from the LLC. The Internal Revenue Service (IRS) classifies LLCs either as partnerships or sole proprietorships depending on the number of owners. Two owners classify as a partnership, while one owner is classified as sole proprietorship. The LLC classification allows you to take advantage of the "pass-through" taxation, so the LLC does not pay any LLC taxes or corporate taxes. As a small business owner, I highly, highly, highly recommend you register your business as an LLC. While I am a firm believer in the LLC, there are many complicated tax laws that affect LLCs and corporations differently. You should do your research and consult a tax professional for your particular situation. There are a lot of benefits to forming an LLC than a corporation as a beginning business ownerIt's also worth pointing out that LLCs can opt (at the start or at a later date) to be taxed by the IRS as either an S- or C-corp, which may offer additional tax benefits for some companies while still maintaining the ease of operating of an LLC versus a corporation. This is as simple as filing the relevant form with the IRS either with the creation of the LLC, or at a later date to reclassify the tax status of the LLC. Consult with your accountant to determine what makes the most sense for your business..

It's also worth pointing out that LLCs can opt (at the start or at a later date) to be taxed by the IRS as either an S- or C-corp, which may offer additional tax benefits for some companies while still maintaining the ease of operating of an LLC versus a corporation. This is as simple as filing the relevant form with the IRS either with the creation of the LLC, or at a later date to reclassify the tax status of the LLC. Consult with your accountant to determine what makes the most sense for your business.

4. Easy on the owner

Running and maintaining a business is hard. The daily grind of ensuring your business operates like a well-oiled machine will be very challenging. You don't need the stress of worrying about additional laws, rules, and regulations. Your focus should be on growing your customer base and maximizing your profit margins. With an LLC, you don't have a fixed management structure that consists of a board of directors overseeing company policies and procedures. You don't want to deal with meeting every year to elect directors and conduct other company business.

5. Financial Control as an LLC

You have the say-so in the way you divvy up the cash to the owners. The distribution of profits aren't required to be dispersed equally or according to ownership percentage. If you have an agreement between with your partner that one partner should receive more of the profits than the other, that's okay. Corporations, on the other hand, do not have this flexibility. Corporations must distribute all profits according to the number of shares each shareholder possess. Owners of LLCs have less stress with taxes, an easier time managing the LLC, and simple record-keeping and reporting requirements as opposed to corporations. I highly recommend you consider registering your business as an LLC!

How to Establish an EIN

When **filing taxes for your business, you will need** an employer identification number (EIN), which consists of nine digits (xx-xxxxxxx). The purpose intended for the EIN is to register the business entity, open a checking account, obtain a business loan (if needed), and gain the trust of vendors. Look at it this way: An EIN is to a business what social security number (SSN) is to a person. If you want your business to be recognized as a real business, you will have to obtain an EIN. The beautiful thing about acquiring an EIN is that it doesn't cost you anything; it's free and doesn't take long to get.

Just because your barbershop or beauty shop isn't some big corporation doesn't mean you shouldn't operate as such. We barbers and beauticians have to get out of the mindset that our business is any less than any other business in the world. You are the business; you are the engine in the car that makes everything go. In my opinion, every small business needs an EIN, and I would advise you to obtain one before your business opens. Having an EIN for your business will help you stay organized when it's time to file taxes and make it easier for your accountant to organize your bookkeeping. I'm going to give you six reasons why you should obtain an EIN for your business:

1. Avoid tax penalties

If you have mixed personal fund with business funds and you do not possess an EIN, you run a high risk of getting yourself in trouble with the IRS. The EIN helps keep everything organized and structured for your accountant and yourself. You should be able to see and recognize the difference in personal transactions and business transactions daily.

2. Stop identity theft

When doing business with clients and vendors, you no longer have to provide them with a social security number—you can use your EIN instead. Therefore, you can keep your SSN private. One of the great things about the improvement of technology in society today is the ability we have to access information so quickly, but, as you already know, there are scam artists out there looking for people to take advantage of. As a boss, you want to do everything possible to protect you and your business from being scammed. By using your EIN, you lessen the chances of a scam artist stealing your personal identity.

3. Establish credibility

In the competitive world of business, you never want to appear as if you're operating as just a side job or hobby. You want everyone you interact with to know you are for real about the goods and services you provide. There are many components in gaining the respect of your business counterparts, and possessing an EIN is one of them.

By obtaining an EIN, you have communicated to the IRS, the public, and potential clients that you have a real business.

4. Acquire business loans

Most lenders require a business banking account that shows your business has been actively doing business transactions over a period of time. These lenders want to ensure your business can sustain a consistent amount of revenue before lending you their cash. Although some lenders don't require you to have an EIN to receive a loan, most do, and having an EIN will look a whole lot better for you when asking a lending institution to lend cash to your business. Also, some lending institutions run credit checks as part of their stipulations prior to lending funds. Having an EIN assists you in building business credit, and without business credit, it will be very difficult to get a business loan unless you have personal cash to guarantee the loan in case of default.

5. Open a business bank account

Most banks have strict policies that require you to have an EIN in order to open a business bank account. So I highly suggest that you, as a business owner, get an EIN as quickly as possible Having a business bank account means you can easily keep all your personal and business transactions separate, which will make your year-end taxes that much easier.

6. Establish business credit

An EIN is the most important factor in establishing business credit. Your business credit history and your personal credit history are very similar. When you pay bills, apply for personal credit cards, and obtain car and mortgage loans, your personal credit is evaluated by the lending institution to see if and how you pay your bills. Do you pay on time? Do you pay at all? Your business credit pretty much operates in the same fashion as your personal credit. Your business has a commercial credit report that is evaluated by lending institutions to see how well your business pays bills—whether your business pays late, on time, or not at all. As a boss, you must continuously monitor the way you're making bill payments for your business. You always want to maintain a good pay history with all of your lenders and vendors. In business, you never know when you might need financial help.

The Importance of an Accountant and a Business Attorney

When opening your barbershop or beauty shop, you may be in a crunch for cash. I understand the struggles of having cash flow in the beginning of a new business adventure. My mother started her first barbershop with a welfare check, and by the grace of God, it worked. Now I'm not recommending you start a business with a welfare check, but I do recommend you try to have some financial stability or money saved up prior to starting. There will be costs involved in starting any business, and you want to be prepared to handle all of the financial obligations headed your way. There are at least two components of your new business that you must have if you are going to last: an accountant and an attorney. In my opinion, these are the pillars of any business earning a substantial amount of cash.

What is an accountant? An accountant is someone who helps you set up the financial structure of your business. An accountant organizes all of your credits and debits and allows you to have a clear vision of your profit margins. An accountant reviews your numbers on a consistent basis and gives you a picture of your daily, weekly, monthly, and annual earnings. An accountant also prepares all of your federal, state, and local tax returns. A good accountant will keep you out of trouble with the IRS and allow you to focus on growing your business and increasing cash flow. You may be able to do most of the day-to-day accounting on your own using simple accounting software like Quickbooks, but I recommend you have an accountant to at least ask questions, review your records, and to assist in filing your taxes.

What is a business attorney? A business attorney will give you clarity on different legal issues regarding your business. A business attorney will help you understand information, rules, laws, policies, and procedures that may affect your business and the way it operates. A business attorney will be able to provide the proper legal guidance needed when you're negotiating contracts and leases. A business attorney is key to approaching challenging legal situations with appropriate counsel.

I'm sure you've heard the saying "Ignorance of the law is no excuse." In business, not knowing something is your own fault. I don't understand the mentality of people who think it's someone else's fault because they didn't know what they needed to know. Listen to me, if you're going be successful in business and in life, the first thing you need to realize is that you are responsible for your outcome. Don't allow yourself not to know information that pertains to the success of your business and the sustainability of your livelihood. You must become an expert in what you do, you must become a student of what you do, and you must become obsessed with what you do! Remember this: The information you don't know, someone does know. Why don't you know the information? Do yourself a favor: Always be resourceful and find out what you need to find out for your own survival.

The Importance of Filing Taxes

In the United States of America, if you are going to make money, there will be an uncle by the name of Sam you will have to answer to. Unfortunately, many people seem to think that filing taxes is something they get to do at their leisure or not at all. Year after year, the IRS assesses penalties and interest for individuals and businesses earning income and not playing by the rules. As a boss, you must understand the importance of filing taxes on time. I'm going to give you three reasons why filing taxes is important for you and your business:

1. It's the law.

If you earn money from working—in any shape, form, or fashion—at some point, you will have to file taxes. The IRS will impose a tax penalty after two years of not filing. You also want to file taxes in order to prove your income to any lending institution.

2. Boss businesses file taxes.

If you want your business to be recognized as a legitimate operation, please make sure you file your taxes on time. Imagine if you saw a business in the news for not filing taxes—how would that make you feel? Would you want to go spend your money there? Of course not; it would make you question their professionalism and wonder if they're shady. The government mandates all individuals and businesses that earn a certain amount of cash annually must file a tax return. Although there are due dates, late filing penalties, and adjustments made by the IRS for tax filers, it would be wise of you to file your taxes on time. Once your taxes have been calculated, one of two things will happen: you will either owe money or you'll receive a refund. Individuals who don't earn the amount of money required by the IRS to have to file taxes, can file voluntarily if they choose to. Filing a tax return is what bosses do. File your taxes and play the game by the rules.

3. Tax returns are required to apply for loans.

If you plan to apply for any type of car loan, mortgage, or traditional loan from any lending institution, there's a great chance they're going to want your last three years of tax returns. These lending institutions want to know how you're going to pay them their money back, and by viewing your tax filings, they can calculate a payment amount suitable for you according to your income. Various economic losses incurred by a business or individual can be used on the tax return as a loss and can benefit the business or individual filing.

One important aspect of running a successful business is having the proper team around you. Please make sure you hire a good accountant/bookkeeper, and business attorney who can teach you all of the rules and regulations of filing taxes.

The Difference Between Personal & Business Banking

As you start to earn money in your business, it's essential that you understand the difference between personal banking and business banking. Before you start accepting or making business-related payments, it's very important to set up a business banking account, separate from your personal checking account. It's imperative you keep your business cash separated from your personal cash, and I'm going to explain why in this chapter.

As the boss, you must understand all of the rules to protect yourself from any negligence. There is no excuse not to know the proper way to establish banking accounts for your business. You must take the time to study the information I'm about to give to you.

When establishing a business checking or savings account, the owner of the business must have business registration paperwork, an EIN, and the name of the business listed on the account in addition to the owner's name. The purpose of the business checking account is to be able to effectively operate the daily tasks of the business, such as writing checks to pay expenses, withdrawing cash, and keeping accurate records of all business-related transactions. Once you have submitted all of the proper documentation to the banker, you will then receive a set of checks and a debit card that will allow you immediate access to your funds. So many times, I've seen barbers and beauticians stick all of their earnings in their front pocket. It's very important to understand the difference between a part-time hustle and a real business! Don't stick all your money in your front pocket; use the proper business banking practices, because it will help you in the long run. We as boss barbers and beauticians must start thinking as CEOs and bosses and not as someone just trying to hustle a quick dollar.

I would advise you to adopt the online banking features which allow you to view your balance at any time, set up automatic payments from your business checking account, and deposit checks via mobile deposit. Also, I would advise you to inquire about overdraft protection features to allow payments to be withdrawn from your account even if the funds aren't there. This generally incurs a fee, but it may be worth having it as a safeguard. And some banks will let you link a savings or another checking account to withdraw from in the instance of insufficient funds, usually without a penalty fee.

Understand that you don't have to establish a business checking account. If you choose to operate as a sole proprietor, you can choose to use your own personal checking account to conduct business transactions. I heartily discourage this practice for a number of reasons; I encourage you to separate your personal account from your business account. Here's why: When servicing or selling goods to a new customer you have no relationship with, just met, and don't know, that particular customer may feel uncomfortable with writing you a check in your personal name. Giving a business name for the customer to pay is more professional than using a personal name. Also, in order to establish a credit score for your business, instead of yourself personally, you will need to have a separate account for your business. The business's credit score is different from the owner's credit score. Finally, you may find accounting and filing taxes much easier when your personal and business transactions are separated.

To my fellow barbers and beauticians: We must begin to conduct our business as if we were in *Forbes* magazine. You are a business, and you need to take pride in what you do. Stop disrespecting your trade, stop allowing other people to disrespect your trade, and conduct your business like a business!

How to Establish Credit When You're Self-Employed

I would first like to congratulate you for taking the time to seek information conducive to your economic growth. You could be watching a TV show right now or playing a video game, but instead, you're in search of a boss way of living.

As a self-employed business owner, you will be faced with the challenge of establishing your own benefits, credit, insurance, and even vacation time. You are in control of your own platform of financial growth, advancement, and lifestyle sustainment. Your financial goals are in your hands, and that's something to be excited about. I want to discuss ways you can establish credit as a self-employed business owner, and other benefits corporate employers use to entice people into working for them and making their financial dreams come true.

Lending institutions have always put self-employed business owners under more scrutiny than regular employees when it comes to getting approved for loans. It's no secret that self-employed business owners have to meet stiffer stipulations when it comes to acquiring a loan of any type. This is why it's so important to educate yourself on the proven ways to establish a good credit rating as an entrepreneur. I'm going to give you four proven ways you can establish credit when you're self-employed.

1. Keep all financial records.

Your accountant is responsible for keeping well-organized spreadsheets of your financial transactions throughout the year. It's imperative you're able to see daily, weekly, monthly, and yearly transaction at all times. Your bookkeeping should be broken down month by month on all debits, credits, and margins of profit. You should always be able to see where your money went and why. Accurate record-keeping will allow you to validate your income and file taxes efficiently.

2. Maintain proof of income.

If you want to receive any type of loan from a lending institution, you will be asked to prove your income. Financial institutions will request documentation proving your income. This is why the practice of well-organized, accurate, precise bookkeeping is so important. When and if you ever have to apply for a loan, you want the comfort of knowing your financial report is accurate and true. You want to be able to show any lending institution the following:

- **Earnings or revenue statement:** The gross income your business made before taxes
- **Expense report:** The total amount of all your expenses
- **Receipts:** Total amount spent on individual transactions, showing where funds were spent

- **Profit and loss statement:** Summarizes all monies spent and earned over a period of time
- **Balance sheet:** Lists all of the assets, liabilities, and investments of your business

When you're able to provide a lending institution a clear vision of your income, it gives you the opportunity to establish good credit with them.

3. Know the credit game.

In order to establish a high credit score, you want to make sure you pay all of your bills on time. Timely payments show a creditor you are responsible and demonstrate that you have good financial habits. Remember, your repayment history is key when establishing credit.

You also want to periodically view your credit report to ensure no mistakes are being made. You may request a free credit report from each of the three credit agencies (Transunion, Equifax, and Experian) once per year at www.annualcreditreport.com.

Another way to improve your credit score is to keep your debt as low as possible. Obtain a secured credit card and use it for all of your expenses, but pay the card in full at the end of the month. You want to show activity in your monthly spending. Try to keep your debt at 30% of your earnings.

Finding a Space to Lease

When starting a new business and leasing a space, you will be required to sign a commercial lease agreement. When signing a commercial lease agreement, you want to ensure clear understanding of everything within the agreement. Don't allow yourself to be taken advantage of by a landlord or leasing agency because you were too lazy to educate yourself on the details of the lease. Leasing retail space can be stressful and time-consuming if you don't prepare yourself. Leasing retail space for your business will be one of the biggest expenses you will encounter. So make sure you take all of the proper steps when making your selection. I'm going to give you some key points to consider when selecting your new place of business, as well as what to look out for before signing a commercial lease.

1. Location, Location, Location

Location is the most important decision you can make when starting a new business. The location will affect many aspects of the way your business operates daily. If you're opening a new barbershop or beauty shop, you want to have as much accessibility as possible in order to gain walk-in clientele. Therefore, your shop should be in a location where there is plenty of drive-by traffic. Ask the person you are leasing from about this before signing the lease. And don't just take their word for it—visit the location at different times and on different days to get a feel for traffic.

Location in a barbershop or beauty shop is the most important factor when starting a new business because you will be retailing products and services directly to the consumer. Wherever your location is going to be—in a freestanding building or a strip mall—you want your potential customers to be able to have easy access to your establishment. Also, being located in an area with a high volume of traffic will give you the ability to market your services with signs, banners, storefront displays, and lighting.

2. Competition

When you open up a new business, you must understand there are going to be other competitors who market and sell similar goods and services. If you can find an area in which you are the only business that offers the service you provide, you have the advantage of being the only option on the block.

3. Parking and Accessibility

You also want to ensure that your potential customers are provided convenient parking spaces. If the location you choose to lease has limited parking space for clients, this could possibly cause you to lose customers. Therefore, when you're looking for potential places to lease, you must keep in mind the amount of parking space available for your customers.

4. Size

It is very important that you measure the square footage of the space you want to lease yourself. Most commercial leases are priced based on the rentable square footage (RSF). This includes the usable square footage (USF). The usable square footage is the actual amount of floor space that can be used. You want to ensure the actual amount of space you're paying for can be used for your intended purposes. If there are common areas shared by you and other tenants, such as lobbies, restrooms, staircases, or hallways, you must take this into consideration when negotiating the price of your lease. You should not have to pay full price for an area that's being shared.

5. Lease Type

When preparing to lease a commercial space, you want to make sure you understand the type of lease you will be entering into. There are two basic lease types I want to give you some insight on before you decide to enter into a commercial lease. A gross lease allows the tenant to pay one large sum of money every month, and then the landlord pays their expenses. A net lease also allows the tenant to pay base a base rent, but the tenant will also have some other expenses to pay as well. In a gross lease, all you have to do is make one payment to your landlord or leasing agency, and the rest of the expenses will be accounted for out of that one payment. In a gross lease, your payment is all-inclusive; the landlord will pay the taxes, insurance, utilities, janitorial services, and maintenance. The tenant is always responsible for their own property insurance and taxes. In my opinion, I would recommend you enter into a gross lease. You will benefit from this type of lease because it will allow you to focus on growing your business. You will not have the responsibility of the building—the landlord will.

Renting a commercial lease space is a huge responsibility. The sustainability of your business may ride on certain conditions of your lease agreement. Before you try to negotiate the terms of a commercial lease agreement with a landlord or leasing agency, make sure you understand all of the details and functionality of a commercial lease. Don't wing it! If you can't seem to grasp the information while reading through a commercial lease, you should consult an attorney to read and explain the lease to you its entirety.

Hiring Contractors for the Build-Out of Your Space

In the United States of America, the construction industry has grown tremendously year after year. With the population increasing at a rapid rate, the need for new homes, new buildings, and new construction is in high demand. Many construction businesses are looking for opportunities to earn income and make your dreams come true. As a boss, you must be able to hire the right company to prepare your space for the operation of your new business. It's imperative that you present your barbershop or beauty shop to the public in a high-class fashion. Customers gravitate toward professional, clean, beautiful places of business. Don't be one of these businesspeople who doesn't understand that you need to spend money with other professionals and you can't do everything yourself. The "I'm going to do everything myself and save every dollar without hiring professional help" mentality will have you out of business lickity-split! Time is money and money is time. You can't do everything; don't even try it. As a boss, it's your job to quarterback your business. Some things you can do yourself, but let someone help you with the things you can't do yourself. Start thinking like a boss. I know what you're thinking right now: "I can save money if I can do it myself." In some situations this is true, but you do not want to waste precious time performing minor tasks or tackling projects beyond your abilities just to save a few bucks. In the long run, you will end up losing money if you're not capable of completing these tasks. This is why you want to ensure you have enough startup capital prior to creating your business.

In my past experiences with contractors, I can tell you mostly all of them have been on the "Shady Grady" side. Let's face it, the true meaning of profit in itself is sketchy. The conceptual meaning of profit is simply producing or providing a product or service for a cost and then monetizing the value for more than it's actually worth. If you really look at it, in order to make a profit off of any goods or services, someone has to give something less valued than the price charged. Ladies and gentlemen, welcome to the world of business! Keep this in mind when hiring any type of contractor to work on your business, home, boat, or car. Here are some warning signs and tricks I want you to be aware of when dealing with contractors. I like to call these behaviors "bananas in the tailpipes."

1. "I'm going to need the money up front for material and supplies before I get started." One of the most common tricks reported to the Better Business Bureau (BBB) is the contractor asking for a percentage or all of the cash up front because they have to purchase materials to start and complete the job. What usually ends up happening is, once the contractor receives the dough, they

vanish on you like Houdini or don't perform the work up to your expectations. Now guess what? You're stuck with this scumbag's work, and they think you're too stupid to sue them because if you were smart you wouldn't have been dealing with them in the first place.

So how do we prevent this from happening? NEVER, NEVER, NEVER give a contractor money up front without doing your research on the contractor and securing a written, legally binding agreement specifying all of the terms of the agreement. And if you do give the contractor money up front, never give more than 10%. When will the work begin? How long will it take? What is the cost of material? What happens if they don't meet your deadline? Who pays for permit costs if needed? Are they a member of the BBB? In the event of a disagreement, who pays court costs? These are just a few questions you need to take into consideration when dealing with contractors. One thing I had to learn the hard way is not to trust anyone in business. Did you hear me? I said DON'T TRUST ANYBODY. I know that sounds harsh, but trust me when I tell you not to trust anyone when doing business. I personally lost close to $800,000 because I trusted someone I shouldn't have. Please be better than me. Don't lose money because you want to trust someone. The reason business is called business is because you're supposed to separate your personal feelings and emotions from business and do everything based on logic and what is best for your operation. The second you start incorporating emotions and feelings into business, you will find yourself out of business.

2. As a boss, you must be able to recognize game. Game is when a person tells you whatever you want to hear or what they think you want to hear in order to get what they want from you. In the beginning, the contractor will be kind, humorous, and very agreeable about doing everything you want done to your specifications. If they are really good at being a scumbag, they will even offer to do extra work and modifications to appease you. This is why you must always have a written contract with all of the details clearly specified. A verbal understanding is no good, because in a court of law, it's your word against theirs. Never take a contractor's word for anything! Remember, business is not about words, it's is about written agreements that can be referred to in the event of a disagreement or breach of contract.

   You need to become an expert in your local state and municipality's regulations before starting on a construction project. Ignorance of the law is not a permissible excuse, and many contractors are not going to be acting in your best interest. A scumbag contractor will tell you they don't need to pull a permit, knowing full well that a permit is legally required for any significant construction project. When performing construction work, every municipality has rules and regulations that all contractors must abide by for safety reasons.

As a boss, it's your responsibility to know all of the permit requirements as pertaining to your business. Don't allow a scumbag contractor to give you false information that could possibly put you out of business; do your homework. Go down to your local city hall and ask for the Building and Permits Department. There, you will be able to gain all the information needed for your build-out and ask any questions you may have. Remember, the scumbag contractor's objective is simple: rob you! They don't care about your business; they only care about making money off of you. It's the responsibility of the contractor to apply for the work permit, because they are the one performing the work. Do not take out a permit for someone else, ever. You don't want to get involved in any dishonest business. Always do business the right way. Anyone trying to get you to do business the slick way doesn't have your best interest in mind, nor do they care anything about your livelihood. Scumbag contractors always try to find a slick way to get around the rules. They will tell you things like, "Oh, don't worry about it, it will be okay, the inspector won't notice." Then, the next thing you know, you're out of business!

To my fellow barbers and beauticians, please listen to what I'm telling you: Don't cut corners, and don't allow someone else to ruin your opportunity for a few dollars. Be firm, forward, and focused. Insist every contractor working for you gets the appropriate building permits, because it lets the governing authority know of your construction project and weeds out all of the scumbag contractors.

3. In the past, I've experienced a contractor quoting me a price which we agreed on, and halfway through the job, he started complaining about how hard the work was and how he should have charged me more money. It gets better—he then refused to finish the work at the price we agreed to and threatened to quit unless I gave him more money. I couldn't believe the nerve of this guy! What a sleazeball! So I kept my composure and simply asked him to finish the work we agreed to at the price we agreed to, and when the work was completed, we could negotiate a smaller increase in the money owed to him. At this point, I was so frustrated I just wanted him out of my shop. Long story short, he finished up the work, I gave him a little extra cash, and everything worked out. My advice to you is that before you sign an agreement with a contractor, make sure you have a "change of work order" clause that states that

any change in the scope of work agreed to will be negotiated and discussed for change of pay.

Always do your research when it comes to hiring contractors. If you look at the word, you will notice the first part is CON. I'm not insinuating that all contractors are scumbags, but I want you to have your antennas up when it's time to hire one.

Marketing and Advertising Your Barbershop or Beauty Salon

Barbering and beautician businesses go against the grain when it comes to the standard business principles taught in colleges across the country. In most business schools or universities, students are taught the importance of marketing, advertising, promotion, increasing profits, location, finance, and all of the technical logistics that go along with implementing good business principles. Even though some of the barbershops and beauty shops across the country implement the standard business principles, some don't, and they are still able to earn income. Why is that?

Black-owned barbershops and beauty shops have always been the heartbeat of the community. The Black-owned beauty and barbershop has always been a place where a customer gets way more than just a haircut or relaxer. "The shop" has always been a place where you may hear political debates, sports analysis, relationship counseling, preaching, teaching, laughing, joking, and much more. The position of the Black-owned barbershop and beauty shop in American culture was presented to the world in 2002 in a film titled *Barbershop*, starring O'Shea Jackson, a.k.a. Ice Cube. The film highlighted the ability of African American men to become entrepreneurs and all of the challenges in running a Black-owned barbershop within the community. In the film, there was never a focus on marketing strategies or how to increase profit margins. Even though standard business practices are practiced in African American barbershops and beauty shops, the key essential factor in determining how a business survives is simple: relationship-building.

In a 2014 *Marketplace* feature on "A History of the African-American Barbershop," Kai Ryssdal and Quincy Mills explain:

> In the 19th century . . . most black-owned barber shops served wealthy, white clients—businessmen and politicians. "The Black barbers were in most cases enslaved men, but also free blacks" . . . Barbering became a way for some African Americans "to find some little pockets to sort of figure out how they could at least earn a little bit of money, and control their time—which of course was what slaves did not have control over." That shifted in the late 1880s and 1890s, when a younger generation entered barbering. They were born after emancipation and specifically opened shops in black communities to serve black men.

So, how did the Black-owned barbershop market and promote during a time of extreme racism and limited opportunity?

Through word of mouth advertising and relationship building, the Black-owned barbershop has always been able go against the grain when it comes to the implementation of standardized business principles. In the late 1880s, when the younger generation of barbers entered into the profession, segregation was at its height, causing Black people to only engage with other Black people within the community. The citizens of the community all shared the same problems and political issues, causing the barbershop to be the hub for open discussions. Customers were allowed to express themselves and talk about anything—the births of their children, favorite singers, sports players, and political views. This open floor of discussion allowed owners and customers to collaborate with one another, which would turn into personal relationships and loyal bonds. There was no internet, marketing agencies, Facebook or Twitter, the key essential factors that drove business to the Black-owned barbershop were relationship building and word-of-mouth marketing. Unlike any other business in America, the foundation of marketing the Black-owned barbershop in the today's world is still the same: relationship-building and word-of-mouth advertisement.

Now, I'm not discouraging Black-owned barbershops shops and beauty salons from implementing successful business principles and practices in their businesses. I'm simply highlighting the two main components that bring economic gain to Black-owned barber and beauty salons across the United States of America.

Most businesspeople will tell you marketing and promotion are important for several reasons. I'm going to give you three reasons why I feel marketing and promoting your barber and beauty business is essential for economic gain.

1. Because of the extremely competitive world we live in, marketing in itself has become big business. Millions upon millions of dollars are spent each year by a variety of businesses to promote their services and products in order earn more revenue. The CEOs of these companies know they're in competition with other companies similar to theirs to gain and retain customers. If you want your beauty or barbershop to consistently earn revenue in today's market, you must market, promote, network, and advertise your business. Marketing is important to gain advantage over other competitors. I would advise you to join your local Business Network International (BNI) group. By becoming a member of a BNI group, you will have access to other businesses in the group that will help you promote your business and increase your profit margins.

2. Through marketing and promotion, you will be able to increase your clientele, identify customer wants, and monetize your products and services. You will have the ability to establish competitive price points that will allow you to sustain your customer base and determine your margins of profit. This insight will give you the tools necessary to ensure your business's sustainability in the marketplace.

3. Marketing is important for personal and business growth. The more visible you make your business to consumers, the more opportunity you will have to build your customer base and increase your profit margins. If you are the CEO of a business, it's imperative to consistently promote your goods and services. You must understand that, while operating a business, every second of the day must be used wisely in your hunt to earn more revenue.

I remember being a teenager heading to college on a football scholarship, and my mother told me I should also consider going to barbering school. At the time, my mind was focused on playing professional football in the NFL. The thought of being a barber seemed like a dramatic drop in career choice for me. I mean, I was considered one of the top 100 high school football players in the country, and my mom thought I should go to barbering school. It made me question her belief in me as a football player. I was too dumb to understand she was preparing me for life after football. Because of her life experiences and wisdom, she knew that sometimes our plans in life don't always pan out. My mom told me, "Son, always have a way you can make your own money, so that no one can fire you." Well, guess what? I would later end up getting hurt in my senior year, and my football career went downhill from there. I had to find a way to bounce back from depression and embarrassment; I had to find myself, because, for the first time in my life, I felt lost.

My momma has always been a hustler, go-getter, and self-promoter. My momma always had an entrepreneur's mindset and was not afraid to take risks. My momma promoted musical talent and held her own concerts, sold cotton candy and corn dogs at local festivals, and owned a beauty salon and barbershop. My mom taught me how to hustle, and I'm so glad she did. Watching her take her hard-earned money and invest in what she believed in gave me the understanding of true independence. Her ability to market and promote allowed her to try different business adventures that inspired her.

When it comes to marketing and promoting your business, you must understand the GRIT and GRIND it takes in order to maximize your earnings. It's very exciting in the beginning of a business venture for most people, because this is the initial phase in which the mental and physical demand hasn't started yet. The energetic planning of the grand opening, the choosing of color designs of uniforms, the selection of the office space, and all of the bells and whistles that come along with the "fun stuff" when starting a business. But, as a boss you must understand the "fun stuff" will be short lived and you will be faced with challenges during the growth and maturation of your business.

I also own a roofing and general contracting company and I've learned the way water travels when a leak is present. Did you know water travels to the places of least resistance? You may be asking yourself, what does how water travels have to do with promoting a business? Let me explain the correlation. Some people always choose the easy way out. These people fall victim to their fear of feeling pain or discomfort. These people choose to live a very safe and risk-free life in order to avoid experiencing heartache or setbacks. These people travel through life like the water in a roof leak, only to the places of least resistance. Don't be like these people! Promoting and marketing your business in my opinion has to be looked at like a heavyweight boxing match. It's you against failure. Who's going to win? Listen, you have to outwork your competitors and push yourself past your own expectation. You have to be a student of your profession and master all of the intricate details that will put you a step above the rest. Here are my top seven ways to promote a barbershop and beauty salon:

1. Social Media Marketing
2. Mailers
3. Neighborhood Door Tags
4. School Calendars Ads
5. BNI Groups
6. Radio Advertisement
7. Youth Sport Organizations

How to Find and Hire
Barbers and Beauticians

One of the most important things you will do when opening your own shop will be selecting people to work with. My advice to you is to screen your potential coworkers as if your livelihood depends on it—because it does!

As a boss, you can't afford to hire incompetent people who don't fit the vision you have for your business. In order to increase your profit margins, you will have to acquire like-minded people. Don't make exceptions. Trust me when I tell you: If you interview people and you know they're not a good fit for your operation, don't hire them!

I've made this mistake before, and it came back to haunt me. One particular time, I hired a barber, and over time, I began to trust him and like him as a friend. Well, one particular Saturday, I asked him to collect my booth rent, and he collected it, alright. The man left town with my money and I didn't hear from him until eight months later. I knew when I hired him I was taking a risk, and sure enough, it came back to bite me.

With all of the social media platforms, it's a lot easier to attract the right barbers and beauticians for your salon. Use platforms like Facebook, Instagram, Indeed, and LinkedIn to inform potential employees about your establishment. You can also post "stylist needed" signs in your actual shop. You would be surprised how well a sign in a window can attract the person you need. If you stick to the principles of the boss mentality, you won't have to worry about attracting employees; they will come to you.

Once you have people wanting to work in your establishment, you'll really need to understand the different ways in which you can hire them. So many barber and beauty shop owners don't realize the tax liabilities that come with certain types of employment.

For instance, if you are hiring a stylist and providing them a salary, wage, or commission, then you will be responsible for tax deductions, workers' compensation insurance, health-care benefits, and payroll taxes.

If you are hiring a stylist and they will be renting a booth, then you will not be responsible for any taxes, health insurance, or benefits. Booth renters are considered independent contractors and are responsible for their own businesses. Booth renters are not employees of yours, even though they operate in your business.

Look at it this way: If you're leasing a space from a landlord, your business is separate from theirs, but you're operating your business within their business. Within the lease you agree to, you will have terms and conditions to abide by. A booth renter operates within your business under the same premise as a lease agreement. Understanding the difference between an independent contractor and an employee can be somewhat confusing. So many barber and beauty shop owners classify new hires incorrectly on their taxes and run the risk of encountering serious tax liabilities with the IRS. However, the IRS has published a guide every person thinking about entering into the barber and beauty profession should reference: "Independent Contractor (Self-Employed) or Employee" on the IRS website, under Small Business and Self-Employed. This will give you an understanding of the difference between an independent contractor and an employee and assist you in deciding how to hire your future stylists.

Here are the three main points that the IRS suggests considering when determining the classification of a worker as either an employee or a contractor:

1. **Behavioral:** Does the company control or have the right to control what the worker does and how the worker does his or her job?

2. **Financial:** Are the business aspects of the worker's job controlled by the payer? (these include things like how worker is paid, whether expenses are reimbursed, who provides tools/supplies, etc.)

3. **Type of Relationship:** Are there written contracts or employee type benefits (i.e., pension plan, insurance, vacation pay, etc.)? Will the relationship continue and is the work performed a key aspect of the business?

Businesses must weigh all these factors when determining whether a worker is an employee or independent contractor. Some factors may indicate that the worker is an employee, while other factors indicate that the worker is an independent contractor. There is no "magic" or set number of factors that "makes" the worker an employee or an independent contractor, and no one factor stands alone in making this determination. Also, factors which are relevant in one situation may not be relevant in another.

The keys are to look at the entire relationship, consider the degree or extent of the right to direct and control, and finally, to document each of the factors used in coming up with the determination.

Acknowledgments

Life gives us the opportunity to be heard or silenced during or after our time has been spent. Some people choose to create and craft a life filled with their heart's desires, while others surrender and accept whatever life throws their way, never to be heard or experience the triumph of self-fulfillment. I have chosen to weather the storms of life, face the difficulties of life, and embrace the pains of life. I'll be the first to tell you it's hard, but it's worth it!

As I sit here and think about my journey thus far and the many learning lessons I've encountered, I'm thankful and humbled to be able to share a part of my story with you. It brings tears to my eyes to reminisce about the days of old and the love my friends and family showed me. I know we aren't supposed to live in the past, but sometimes I feel it's necessary to remember our past in order to move forward into tomorrow. I have a very good memory and I remember the people that took the time to talk with me, laugh with me, share with me, and comfort me in my time of need.

I dedicate this book to: my KINLOCH FAMILY; my next-door neighbors, Inez and Buster Peebles; my neighbors James A. Robinson and Florence Robinson; my childhood barber and friend, Lucious; my two best friends for life, Martinez Robinson and John Easely; and my two sisters, Mona Patterson Hughes and Rochelle Patterson Lampkin. But most of all, I dedicated this book to my momma, Anita L. Patterson.

I grew up in a single-parent household with my two sisters and my mom. I watched my mom sacrifice her own personal wants and needs to provide for us. My mother sold cotton candy, cleaned office buildings, and opened a beauty salon and a barbershop. My mother told me to "Always have a way to make your own money." She is the reason why I'm the entrepreneur and man I am today. I believe when God was assigning mothers to sons, He knew we would be the perfect match. Love you, Momma.

Listen to me, I'm living proof that anything is possible in this life! I understand in life there's a beginning and an end. If you're reading this book, you still have life left in your body. Go for your dreams, don't settle for average, give effort in everything you do! I hope you can learn from my mistakes and accomplishments and live your best life. I love you all and thank you.

Raymond M. Patterson Jr.

About the Author

RAYMOND M. PATTERSON JR. owns Cut Styles and More, a successful barbershop in St. Louis, Missouri, as well as a roofing and general contracting company. He made his first million dollars through barbering and is a motivational speaker. His other professional pursuits include instructing barber college, teaching elementary and high school students, producing music, owning a trucking company, and more. Patterson received his bachelor's degree from University of Missouri-St. Louis and his master's in education administration from Missouri Baptist University, as well as being certified in physical training, health, and education administration. He earned football scholarships to Northern Illinois University, where he set seven records and was a nationally ranked kick returner, and Memphis State University, where he set a record 40-yard dash and played alongside Isaac Bruce. He was selected to play in the European Football League in Nuremberg, Germany. He credits the grace of God for his life's accomplishments. *The Million Dollar Barber* is Patterson's first book for adults; *Little Life Skills* was his first children's book.

Throughout life's trials and tribulations, he has always kept fighting to be successful and to make his mother proud. He grew up in the streets of Kinloch, Missouri, with the guidance of his mother encouraging him to strive for greatness. His purpose in life is to motivate, encourage, and inspire the people in need of the world. Patterson is a fan of the underdog; he loves a comeback story and making something out of nothing. As you read through the pages of his creation, recognize and utilize the and life lessons—borne from his own experiences—he has provided for you.

Personal Accomplishments

High School

- All-state running back at McCluer North High School
- Record holder in the 400-meter dash in track and field
- Blue chip football player
- Named in Top 100 Players in *Lindy's Sports* magazine

University

- Received football scholarship to Northern Illinois University
- Set 7 records freshman year
- Freshman All-American/Northern Illinois
- Nationally ranked kick returner at Northern Illinois University
- Started as KR, WR, RB, and PR after transfer to Memphis State University
- Played alongside Isaac Bruce (wide receiver for the St. Louis Rams and San Francisco 49ers)

- Ran a record 4.32" 40-yard dash at Memphis State University
- Selected to play in EPL (European Football League) in Nuremberg, Germany
- Bachelor's degree in general studies, University of Missouri-St. Louis
- Master's degree in education administration, Missouri Baptist University
- Certified in physical education, health, and education administration

Professional

- Owner, Cut Styles and More barbershop
- Barber license and barber instructor license
- Author, *Little Life Skills* children's book
- Motivational speaker: the Pharmacist
- CEO of RMP Roofing and General Contracting, LLC
- Elementary school teacher
- Former CEO of F&P Investments, LLC
- Former CEO of F&P General Contractors, LLC
- Former CEO of the University of Barbering/ Barber College, LLC
- Former CEO of Base Hit Investments, LLC
- Former CEO of Grind Up Records, LLC
- Former CEO of CSM Transportation, LLC
- Former CEO of Champions Logistics and Delivery Services, LLC

- Former high school teacher
- Former general contractor
- Former real estate investor
- Former member of Naturally Smooth, an R&B singing group
- Former part-owner of Deez Beats production company
- Former self-made millionaire

Made in the USA
Las Vegas, NV
19 December 2022

63545994R00073